DATE			

NORWAY

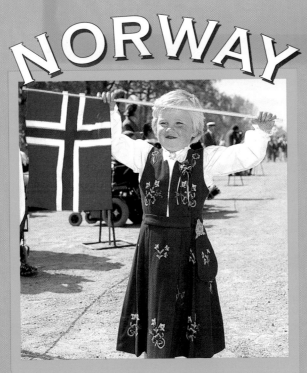

A TRUE BOOK

by
Elaine Landau

Children's Press®

A Division of Grolier Publishing

New York London Hong Kong Sydney
Danbury, Connecticut

Hedmark, Norway

Reading Consultant
Linda Cornwell
*Coordinator of School Quality
and Professional Improvement
Indiana State Teachers
Association*

Author's Dedication
For Jayson Garmizo

**Visit Children's Press® on the
Internet at:
http://publishing.grolier.com**

Library of Congress Cataloging-in-Publication Data

Landau, Elaine.
  Norway / Elaine Landau.
    p.   cm. — (True Book)
  Includes bibliographical references and index.
  Summary: Provides an overview of Norway, describing its history,
geography, climate, and culture.
    ISBN: 0-516-20985-X (lib. bdg.)   0-516-26767-1 (pbk.)
    1. Norway—Juvenile literature. [1. Norway.] I. Title. II. Series.
DL409.L36   1999
948. 1—dc21   98-37714
                                                        CIP
                                                        AC

GROLIER
PUBLISHING

Contents

A tourist takes a daring peek at the scenery below.

A Special Place

Picture a northern land with a rugged mountainous beauty all its own—a place of evergreen forests, glaciers, sparkling lakes, and waterfalls. The long narrow inlets of the sea known as fjords frequently cut into the coastline. If you haven't already guessed, this land of deep valleys and tall cliffs is Norway.

Norway is a country located in the northwestern area of Europe called Scandinavia. Norway, Denmark and Sweden, are known as Scandinavian countries.

Norway occupies an area of 125,181 square miles (324,218 square kilometers). It is bordered by the Barents Sea to the north, the Norwegian Sea and the North Sea to the west,

and Skagerrak Strait to the south. Finland, Sweden, and Russia are on the east.

A third of Norway lies above the Arctic Circle. This northern portion of the nation is sometimes called the "Land of the Midnight Sun." That's because it lies so far north that from about mid-May to the end of June, the sun never sets. Norway has sunlight twenty-four hours a day. Then, from the end of

November through the end of January, the sun doesn't rise above the horizon. During this season, it's dark all day.

Although Norway is about as far north as Alaska, its coastal region tends to be warmer. The warm North Atlantic Current of the Gulf Stream keeps the climate mild. The warmer tempera-tures usually keep the fjords from freezing and allow the

Although temperatures can reach as low as 5 degrees Fahrenheit (-15 degrees Celsius) along the coast, this harbor remains free of ice.

snow to melt more quickly. Even during the coldest months of the year, most of Norway's harbors are ice free. However, things change as you move inland from the coast. The weather is colder there, and snow often covers much of the ground. The temperature on Norway's southern coast might be 45 degrees Fahrenheit (7 degrees Celsius) in January, but inland winter temperatures of 0 degrees Fahrenheit (-18 C) are not unusual.

But regardless of the climate, Norway offers us a vivid view of nature's splendor. Of the three Scandinavian

A wintry Norwegian morning at the Royal Palace

countries, Norway is often said to have the most breathtaking scenery.

Norwegians

The Norwegian people tend to be tall and have fair coloring. But they are not all blond and blue-eyed, as is sometimes thought. Norwegians are close-ly related to the Scandinavian people in nearby Sweden and Finland, as well as the citizens of Denmark and Iceland.

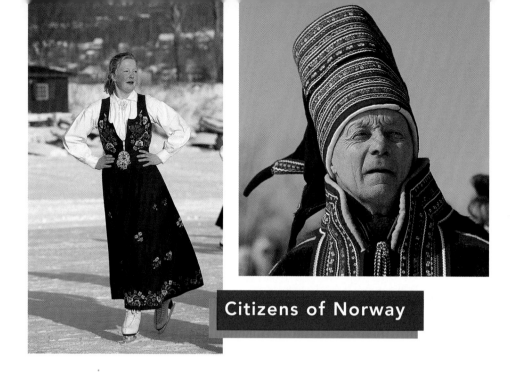

Citizens of Norway

The only large minority group in Norway are the Lapps. The Lapp people live in Lapland—a very cold region that stretches across Norway, Sweden, Finland, and northern Russia above the Arctic Circle. Most Lapps are small people with high cheekbones and straight dark hair. However, many Lapps marry Scandinavians, and their offspring are a blend of both groups.

In the past, most Lapps raised reindeer herds. Today, they often make their living by fishing or farming. Some Lapps work in cities as well. Norway also has

The mountain Lapps live in northern Norway, where they continue to practice traditional customs such as reindeer herding.

some people of Finnish descent, along with a number of immigrants from Iran, Turkey, Africa, Southeast Asia, the United States, and other countries.

With only about 4.5 million people, Norway has one of the smallest populations in Europe. More than a quarter of the people live in rural areas. Other Norwegians make their homes in cities in the southeast, and on the southwestern coast.

Oslo, the capital and largest city, is Norway's industrial

Oslo was originally named "Christiania" after King Christian IV. It was later renamed Oslo in 1924.

and cultural center. Oslo has a population of more than 480,000 people. The citizens of Oslo and other surrounding cities enjoy a high standard of living. Most of Norway's cities are clean and free of poverty. Many city people own small vacation homes on the coast or in the mountains.

Sports

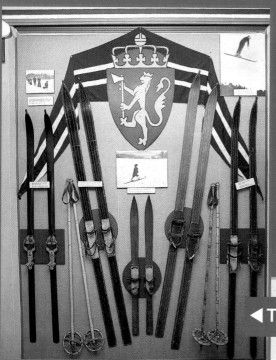

◄The Oslo Ski Museum

Outdoor sports are very popular in Norway. As might be expected, skiing is the national sport. Norwegian children often

▲ Skiers take to the mountains.

in Norway

learn to ski soon after they start walking. Ice skating and cross-country skiing are favorite sports too. Many Norwegians also enjoy soccer, fishing, sailing, and hiking through the country's scenic hills and forests during the summer months.

A fly fisherman enjoys a successful day on the stream. ▼

Norwegian favorites (clockwise from top left): sardine, chicken, and mushroom-and-cheese sandwiches

While people in the United States usually eat three meals a day, most Norwegians eat four or five smaller meals. Generally, they have only one hot meal. Open-faced sandwich of herring, goat cheese, or sliced meat on thin crisp bread are frequently prepared for other times. Fish is an important item in the Norwegian diet too. It is a tra-ditional part of the koldtbord—a selection of tasty cold dishes.

The Evangelical Lutheran Church is the nation's official church, but Norwegians enjoy freedom of religion, and many other faiths are practiced there.

Ninety percent of the Norwegian population belong to the Evangelical Lutheran Church.

The country's official language is Norwegian, which has two similar forms—Bokmal and Nynorsk. These are slowly being combined into a single language.

Nearly all Norwegians can read and write. After high school, students may attend one of the country's colleges or technical trade schools. In addition to its public school system, each Norwegian town or city is required to have a free public library.

Fishing, Farms, and Factories

Much of Norway's economy has thrived and grown in recent years. Its natural resources provide many different types of work, so the country's unemployment rate is fairly low.

Norway's waters have always been important. Cod, herring,

Fishing (left) and the discovery of oil and gas beneath the ocean (below), have helped make Norway's economy one of the strongest in the world.

and mackerel are plentiful, and many people work in the fishing industry.

The nation's water resources have boosted Norway's economy in other ways as well. Since the 1970s, Norwegians have mined the petroleum and natural gas fields that lie offshore in the North Sea. Many swiftly moving rivers in the mountain areas have been used to produce hydroelectric power.

Manufacturing is also a major industry in Norway. Its factories produce petroleum and chemical products, packaged foods, and such metals as aluminum and magnesium. Products from Norway's forests include timber, paper, and many other items.

Only a small portion of the land is used for farming. Much of Norway's terrain is rocky and its soil is somewhat poor. Many Norwegian farmers raise

A farmer tends to his land.

livestock such as cattle, goats, and sheep. The crops produced are mainly used for cattle feed. However, potatoes, barley, wheat, and rye are also grown in Norway.

The Past and the Present

Thousands of years ago, Norway was covered by a thick blanket of ice. As the ice melted, a series of Germanic tribes settled there. They were followed by fierce fishing bands and pirates who became known as Vikings.

The Age of the Viking lasted from about A.D. 800 to 1100. During this period, Scandinavian Vikings sailed the Atlantic Ocean in large ships to steal, rob, and conquer other lands. Spurred by a growing land shortage at home, some Norwegian Vikings settled in Iceland and Greenland. A few Vikings were even more daring. An explorer named Leif Ericson arrived in North America about five hundred years before Christopher Columbus.

Meanwhile, the small independent groups that existed in Norway had begun to

It is believed that Leif Ericson discovered North America in A.D. 1000.

King Olav II established the Church of Norway in 1024. He was later declared a saint in 1164.

unite. King Olav II, who died in 1030, united the country and established Christianity there. Norway became especially wealthy and powerful in the 13th century under King Haakon IV, but then things went badly for the country. Foreign trade losses hurt the economy, and a terrible plague known as the Black Death killed half of Norway's people.

Following the death of the Norwegian king's last descendant in 1319, both Norway and Sweden were jointly controlled by a Swedish king. In 1397, Norway came under

Danish rule, where it would remain until 1814, when Denmark lost it to Sweden through war.

Although the Norwegians accepted the Swedish king, they drew up their own democratic constitution and largely governed themselves. They were granted full independence from Sweden in 1905. Norway remains free and self-governing to this day.

The Government

Norway is governed by a constitutional monarchy. This means that the nation has a monarch—a king or queen—as well as a parliament or law-making body. Norway's parliament is known as the Storting.

The Norwegian monarch has very little power. Governing is

Norway's parliament (above) is situated in the country's capital, Oslo. Prime Minister Gro Harlem Brundtland (right) served as Norway's first woman prime minister from 1981 to 1996.

left to the parliament, whose members are elected for a four-year term. Norway also has a prime minister whose job is much like that of the U. S. president. The prime minister works closely with the Cabinet or Council of State. Cabinet members are also members of parliament. They help determine government policies for the nation.

Through the years, Norway's government has pioneered some important advances. Norway was one of the first countries to give women the right to vote. The Norwegian government also provides financial aid to the elderly, handicapped, orphans, and others with special needs. Under Norway's 1987 National Insurance Act, all the people get free hospital care, doctor's visits, and prescription drugs. Following Norway's example, other countries have adopted similar measures.

The Arts

In addition to its other achievements, Norway has contributed to the world's culture and art. Playwright Henrik Ibsen, often referred to as the father of modern drama, was Norwegian. Three Norwegian writers—Bjornstjerne Bjornson, Knut

Bjornstjerne Bjornson
was awarded the
Nobel Prize for
Literature in 1903.

Hamsun, and Sigrid Undset—
have been awarded the
Nobel Prize for literature.

Outstanding Norwegian
artists and musicians include
sculptor Gustav Vigeland,
whose work has been praised
internationally, and the
famous composer Edvard
Grieg. Grieg's music is highly
regarded throughout the
world.

Undeniably, this northern
wonderland has much to

Henrik Ibsen
(1828–1906)

Henrik Ibsen was one of the greatest playwrights in the world. Born in Skien, Norway, Ibsen published his first play at the age of twenty-two.

Some of his greatest works include: *A Doll's House*, *Ghosts*, *Hedda Gabler*, and *The Wild Duck*. Henrik Ibsen died on May 23, 1906.

This photo of Henrik Ibsen was taken shortly before his death in 1906.

The Lofoten Islands are one of the many spectacular sights to see while in Norway.

offer. With its scenic beauty, outdoor sports, and artistic spirit, Norway has something for everyone.

To Find Out More

Here are some additional resources to help you learn more about the nation of Norway:

Books

Hoobler, Dorothy. **The Scandinavian American Family Album.** Oxford University Press, 1997.

Millard, Anne, consulting ed. **Explorers & Traders.** Time-Life Books, 1996.

Pearson, Anne. **The Vikings.** Viking, 1994.

Penny, Malcolm. **The Polar Seas.** Raintree Steck-Vaughn, 1997.

Pitkanen, Matti A. **The Grandchildren of the Vikings.** Carolrhoda Books, 1996.

Introducing Norway

http://www.dep.no/ud/publ /96/norway/index.html

This site introduces visitors to the culture, geography, environment, and history of Norway.

Let's Go Around the World

http:www.ccph.com

This four-section website takes visitors on a trip from the alps of Norway to the grasslands of Africa and beyond. You'll meet children from different cultures, encounter exotic animals, and much more.

Scandinavian: Nordic Music Festival at Rootsworld

http:www.rootsworld.com/ scanfest/index.html

Follow links to various Scandinavian countries and discover articles, musicians, and some of the hottest music in Europe today.

A Taste of Norway: Recipes for Children

http:odin.dep.no./ud/pub1 /97/nortaste/en/children. html

Maintained by the ODIN Ministry of Foreign Affairs, this site provides favorite Norwegian recipes for children to prepare on their own.

Yahooligans! Around the World: Countries: Norway

http:www.yahooligans.com /Around_the_World/ Countries/Norway/

This fun-filled page provides links to a variety of websites about Norway. From the flags of Norway to a virtual tour of the Northern Lights Planetarium, this is a site you won't want to miss!

Important Words

hydroelectric power electricity developed from water power

immigrant someone who comes to a new country to settle there

koldtbord an assortment of traditional Norwegian dishes served at lunch or dinner

Nobel Prize for Literature an award given annually for the best literary work of the year

offspring children

rural having to do with the countryside

Index

Meet the Author

Popular author Elaine Landau worked as a newspaper reporter, an editor, and as a youth services librarian before becoming a full-time writer. She has written more than one hundred nonfiction books for young people, including many books for Franklin Watts and Children's Press. Ms. Landau, who has a bachelor's degree in English and journalism from New York University and a master's degree in library and information science from Pratt Institute, lives in Miami, Florida, with her husband and son.